Eternal Abundance – An inspirational book to help with the journey of growth. By Cara Barilla

ISBN 9780645285130

Copyright Cara Barilla 2022

All rights reserved Cara Barilla

Published by Little Lemon Book Co.

SYDNEY

www.LittleLemonBookCo.com.au

Graphic Art illustrations by Cara Barilla Graphic

Art Editor by Jessica Chaplin

www.JessChaplinCreative.com.au

www.CaraBarillaAuthor.com.au

This Book is available for your group or organisation. For more information please contact

Little Lemon Book Co. AUS.

Printed in Australia

No part of this publication may be reproduced in whole or in part, or stored in a retrieval system or transmitted in any form or by any means, electronic, mechanical, photocopying, recording or otherwise without written permission of the publisher.

GENRE: Self-help / New age / Spiritual / Gift Book / Quotation Little

Lemon Book Co. First Edition 2022.

An Inspirational book to help with the journey of growth

By Cara Barilla

Dedicated for my Brother Stevie.

Thank you for showing the world that Abundance is Eternal through passion and heart.

"Thank you God for giving me so much more than I could ask for."

"I am grateful eternally and feel the everlasting flow of abundance."

"I am feeling the everlasting source of positive energy."

"Blessings are only given in the present."

"When you feel grateful, you will feel like your energy is limitless."

"Dreams which you believe in can become instant reality."

"Meditation clears the mind and opens a window for manifestation."

"I feel the powerful flow of abundance pulling into my life."

"Your surrounds will prove to you that thoughts will create."

"The greatness of a single thought starts with a dream and ends in reality."

"Thank you for allowing me to create anything I could ever wish for."

"You are either the master or prisoner of your Daydreaming."

"Thank you for giving me the gift of eternal fulfilment."

"The wealthiest heart is forever satisfied."

"My needs are eternally nurtured and I am thankful."

"Gratitude is a portal of creation."

"The true knowingness of pure happiness is the key to everlasting abundance; Where that key is hidden is deep in the present."

"Rich in heart is the pathway to abundance."

"Whatever you wish for will come to you when you offer yourself belief."

"The greatest gift is the present."

"Manifesting abundance is feeling purely abundant."

"When there is everlasting happiness and gratitude; Abundance lives."

"Healing others will feed abundance; As the energy of gratitude of others will be transferred to you."

"Karma will heal and guide you to see what you already can be grateful for."

"Everyone already has abundance; To unlock the energy is deeply hidden in gratitude."

"You are an infinite source of gratitude; don't be afraid to lose energy."

"The source is infinite; The only thing which is stopping you is belief."

"Valuing yourself is a key to inner riches."

"Never wait for perfection to act on your dreams as perfection is simply a state of satisfaction."

"Allow the beauty of presence to shine you with self-happiness."

"Harnessing the emotions that are swimming in gratitude is where you will channel abundance."

"When you realise that your happiness is enough is when you are in eternal abundance."

"The feeling of peace after completion is another portal to self-growth. This will also grow with self-nurture."

"You are enough."

"To find riches physically is to first find riches mentally and soulfully."

"When you forgive yourself, you are allowing positive abundance to flow inside
your mind; And manifest itself into reality."

"Placing your mind into a peaceful state is laying in a bed of abundance."

"You deserve the right to have your own kind of happiness. When you live in your unique world of happiness you will be forever abundant."

"When abundance comes your way always remember to appreciate the present moment in which this energy resides."

"Gratitude plants seeds for success."

"Abundance is to never look and compare with other people's gains."

"When we are in the state of abundance, nothing else is in the way of our goals."

"Creation is infinite when you are a creator."

"If you can't shift your situation, shift your mood. New opportunities may prevail itself."

"You are destined to receive your hearts' desire; If that is what your heart feels is the right circumstance for you at the present moment."

"You are in control of what you fear. The release of fear allows abundance to flow in your mind and heart."

"Giving is an act of abundance."

"Feeling happiness and gratitude will forever flow back to you."

"You are energy. You can manifest anything you wish, if you'll allow and accept it to."

"Visualisation of where you want to be is a dream and a physical shift away."

"When you release daily tensions you are asking the universe to make room for abundance."

"True peace and quiet in the mind allows room for abundance to flow in."

"It's time to let go of all that doesn't serve you and deserve you."

"When your mind is forever flowing in imaginative ideas, positive feelings, healing thoughts and empathy; You are a power source for abundance."

"May you value your worthiness of infinite abundance."

"When you realise that you are not the same person as you were yesterday is a true gift to yourself; The gift of the evolving soul. You are ready."

"I can manage large successes."

"The most powerful tool one can use for abundant growth is wisdom in their heart, kindness in their eyes and compassion in their actions."

"Allow your life to unfold at the right pace. Force will always cause tension and resistance."

"Nurture your physical, emotional and spiritual levels of abundance from your heart, outwards."

"Conceal your wishes close to your heart and watch yourself create magic."

"Don't be scared to walk into the light and shine."

"When you truly want something, the universe will always make sure the opportunities are along your path."

"You are divinely connected to light and will always remain in bliss if you connect to pure heart."

"I am grounded to my life purpose and will abundantly rise."

"May the power of wealth flow to you."

"Seeing all that is great in your life is the root of abundance."

"Abundance isn't something we physically look for; But something we tune our frequency to."

"Giving is a pillar for great abundance."

"Love is your map to self-success."

"Don't forget to count your precious blessings each day; Whether it be the love you have, your protection or even the breath in your lungs."

"Abundance flows alongside love and passion for life."

"Align our frequency with peace, light and love. This is true Abundance."

"Abundance is merely a feeling in your heart guiding your mind."

"Allow gratitude to surround you like a shield."

"Allow your body to be the compass of your destiny; It will always know the way."

"To act in abundance is simply a dare to yourself; Dare to step out of your comfort zone & to think and feel differently."

"Abundance is already inside you. You just need to tune in the right channel."

"Trying to turn your dream into reality isn't about waiting for the dream; But being grateful that you are already a dream."

"Sometimes in order to let new good in, you must release what no longer serves you good."

"I am ready to receive all opportunities of abundance."

"The dreams of your hearts' desire are forever eternal. Don't ever believe you have missed your opportunity; Simply breathe and try again."

"I am forever grateful for the positive flow of energy that repeats in my life".

"And you are just a single thought away from a new lifestyle."

"Hope is the pure essence of positive momentum."

"Thank yourself each day for getting through the last."

"You are a powerful creator. When you truly realise this you can shape your surroundings to your desires."

"When we heal our own traumas, we create powerful healing energy which will serve good for existence. This is how abundance thrives."

"The true source of abundance is waiting to be brought into physical reality. Channel into your light source."

"The healer in you is capable of creating many lights of love. This wealth of healing is abundant."

"Abundance is the greatest gift; For it is a physical form of your gratitude and faithfulness to your soul."

"Kind actions are felt, delivered and shared from the heart and transformed into physical reward."

"Abundance is a physical feeling that has transformed into your physical reality through love and blessings to yourself."

"Abundance is knowing you have served good and seeing the good around you
in physical form;
Cradled by gratitude."

"The quality of your surroundings depend on healthy thoughts, and the quality of your thoughts depend on healthy surroundings."

"When you physically step into the reality of where you want to be, you are physically tuning in to another frequency and bringing your abundance to life."

"Your higher consciousness knows your hearts desires;
It's up to you to soulfully thank your present state in order to deliver you desire."

"There are many blessings in every day. What are the blessings today which you are grateful for?"

"The creator within you wants to create, but can never create in any comfort zone or space that needs to be let go of first."

"When you ask yourself for something, make sure you believe it's already yours;
For the true door to many pathways is self-belief."

"Where your headspace rests is what you will create."

"One of the hardest things to do may be to let go.. The unexpected is always ahead with plenty of room to grow."

"Believing in yourself is a key to abundance."

"Just remember; Its okay to say yes to yourself and no to others. Allow time to heal and recover at your own pace.

This is a piece of soul-growth."

"When you quiet your mind, your soul will sing."

"When you focus on the things which you cannot control only leads you to a cycle you can't remove yourself from."

"Think of the things which you can heal, create and nurture."

"Sometimes when you grow it may feel lonely; Self nurture will not only heal you but guide you to the same frequencies within people."

"Allow yourself to release toxic energies from your mind. When we release, we are giving ourselves love to grow and evolve."

"When we meditate, we can guide our soul to new awakenings, dimensions and people that will help us along the way."

"Never let fear keep you frozen in your comfort zone."

"Always remember; There's a difference between Comfort-zones and Safe-Zones. Comfort-zones can hold us against moving forward, while safe-zones are shields which
protect us along the way."

"Be your own light; Say light-filled words to yourself and watch yourself evolve; As self-nurture will always heal and protect us to the right path."

"Create more; To learn more about our soul patterns."

"Giving is an artful service which Earth-Angels can never live without."

"You are more important than you could ever imagine. Allow your inner dreams to come to life and imprint your magical legacy here on earth."

"Asking yourself out loud where you should be during this pathway through
lifetime will be given to you."

"Your current state always has potential for new beginnings. Your passion is eternal and to relight the passion you must always look outside your comfort zone."

"When you ask for directions in life the road will appear... Like magic."
"And all life is...

A wish granted from Gratitude and Light."

"A lifetime of happiness is a lifetime of gratitude." Healing from within is the secret to an abundant tomorrow."

"Magic can grow from anywhere, as long as there is someone to nurture it."

"When we stop and recover our emotions, clarity will appear, and you will see your true path."

"Don't be afraid to say no to comfort zones;
As it may be our forever confinement."

"The most powerful way to abundance is when we connect to our inner child; We allow our purest dreams to steer to success."

"Don't forget to meditate in gratitude for those who never believed in you; they are the horsepower for our drive to success."

"Your minds current state today is your emotions for tomorrow."

"Harness power by healing small unfinished business. It is the glue that holds the larger pieces together."

"Clear your energy and the negative surroundings. You have so much room for good, so don't waste your sacred space on the negative."

"When we reward ourselves for our small gains, we are reminding ourselves that we are just getting started."

"Reminiscing is forever healing; When we remember the moments when we never had abundance, we are cherishing and enriching our fortunate present."

"What is your dream? When you meditate on your dream in clear, visualise all your senses being there and coming to life… This is guiding manifestation into our near tomorrow."

"Forgiving others without expecting an apology, is a powerful soul ascension and will help you to tune into high frequencies."

"You are always walking in success because you are the success."

"I receive the everyday miracles in my life and I'll never forget how lucky I am."

"No matter what path lies ahead of you; Always live in your true authentic self and nature.
This is where your abundance will live long in this world."

"Grow in faith; Thrive in abundance."

"Everything I desire I already have."

"Self-love is pure magic; You can attract the whole universe in the palm of your hand at an instant when you love and believe in yourself."

"Self-belief is magnetising eternal abundance."

"Step into your power and channel self-love."

"Don't forget to always accept new abundance with self-value."

"You deserve every piece of abundance that comes to you."

"Allow your rewards to grow in the present."

"To appreciate that you have the gift of life is abundant."

"You deserve what is delivered to you."

"When abundance arrives, let it thrive and grow."

"Live in slow motion
with every piece of
abundance
you have; It will eternally
grow."

"You are deserving of pure abundance."

"You are capable of greatness."

"Your mind is your biggest asset and can create anything you want."

"You are capable of turning your dreams into a lifetime
of physical abundance."

"Where dreamers live is where abundance is born."

"The imagination is where the ingredients of pure abundance is designed and delivered from."

"Your heart can guide your manifestation to the right pathways in this reality. Just believe it will happen."

"Soul growth is a sign of physical change."

"Magic is the force of abundance."

"The key to growth is self-belief and valuing yourself greater than the universe. As you can create a whole new galaxy."

"When you make the conscious change to tune into a higher frequency, greater opportunities will flow into your life."

"Don't forget to use your heart at the moment of the need of others and never forget to protect your heart at the moment of self-need."

"Allow good deserving things to happen for you through self-acceptance. This is your time."

"Accepting all that is good
for you and feeling that
you
deserve this and more;
Is pure self-value."

"Hope lives in your heart; Expect great things for you and you will attract that high greatness in vibration and frequency."

"This is a message for you to let go of any heavy energy that you are holding on to. This is your moment to consciously evolve."

"Leaving your comfort zone doesn't always mean physically; Sometimes if you are physically there and don't see chances or change, means you need to mentally & physically shift out of your comfort zone."

"When you open your eyes and heart to wholesome living you are physically living in a place of gratitude."

"When we heal our own heart, we are allowing ourselves to grow from the inside, out".

"Healing is forever shifting. In order to grow and heal yourself you must also help to heal and grow the less fortunate of your surroundings."

"Sometimes when you give back to the community wholeheartedly, you are giving a little bit of wholesomeness back to your heart."

"Patience is the utmost important ingredient of abundance. When you are a patient and kind human, happiness is easy to be seen."

"The largest tree in the woods is merely a seed with
an abundance of support and a nurturing environment."

"Abundance can be found anywhere to the light soul."

"Use your inner gut as a compass to determine what feels right, and what needs to change. Your soul health needs nurture too."

Remember; There are many fails to a great success and many fails after a great success.

Shifts are meant to be."

"Happiness is magnetic; Whether it be in business, love or pleasure."

"It's best to always follow your heart; You can never run away from it so it's best to always follow and listen to your purest guide."

"Forgiving others who have done you wrong is a powerful step to abundance. This allows you to release the old energy to
make room for the new and good."

"If you are feeling a heavy energy at the moment, please treat it as only temporary, then it will release. Whatever you expect as long-term will be there as long as you truly believe."

"What do you feel is good and pure in your heart? This will help support the running fuel to your success."

"I attract all good energies for spiritual growth support."

"Listen to your inner voice and always be kind to yourself inside your thoughts; You are worthy."

"Allow yourself to recharge in your own unique way."

"We all need a healthy energy flow in order to keep going.

Nurture your heart and needs."

"I accept that I can't grow without change; I will step out of my comfort zone for the better of my soul's growth."

"Changing your cycle is changing your behaviour patterns."

"I am a sovereign being and i will shift my energy into this abundant energy field."

"Thank you god for giving me pure sight to the dimension of abundance."

"Your mind holds the control to abundance. Your heart holds the map."

"The frequency within the present will show you never-ending possibilities."

"Your self-value is measured by your own self-belief;

Belief is eternally limitless."

"When you fight for the good in justice, you will be rewarded."

"Once you heal your heart you can open up self-belief to unlimited dreams."

"You are your sole creator; Whatever good you dream for will be offered to you within many discreet pathways and opportunities."

"When you release fear, you open up space for growth within many new pathways."

"Have faith in light; There is positive everywhere if you focus on it."

"I am an eternal power that can re-write my path at any time."

"I will always follow the light and my heart to eternal growth."

"Use the unique wisdom of your heart to guide you to your true-life path."

"When you live in pure heart, you can connect to the heart of the universe."

"The warmth in your eyes can transform the chaos in the world to care & compassion. These are some of the many angelic tools of abundance."

"Magic lives in the heart of chance."

"Combining patience and gratitude can create abundance."

www.ingramcontent.com/pod-product-compliance
Lightning Source LLC
Chambersburg PA
CBHW060647150426
42811CB00086B/2450/J